TIME TO END DEMOCRACY

Abhijit Naskar is the twenty-first century Neuroscientist whose contributions in Cognitive and Behavioral Neuroscience have helped the world tackle the issues of mental illness, prejudice, hate, extremism, discrimination and segregation more effectively. As an untiring advocate of mental health and universal acceptance, he became a beloved best-selling author all over the world with his very first book "The Art of Neuroscience in Everything". With his pioneering ventures into the Neuropsychology of beliefs and biases, he has hugely contributed in the eradication of religious and cultural differences in our world, for which he is popularly hailed as a humanitarian scientist, who takes the human civilization in the path of sweet general harmony.

TIME TO END
DEMOCRACY
THE MERITOCRATIC MANIFESTO

ABHIJIT NASKAR

Time To End Democracy: The Meritocratic Manifesto

An Amazon Publishing Company, 1st Edition, 2020

Printed in the United States of America

ISBN: 9798690037000

Also by Abhijit Naskar

The Art of Neuroscience in Everything
Your Own Neuron: A Tour of Your Psychic Brain
The God Parasite: Revelation of Neuroscience
The Spirituality Engine
Love Sutra: The Neuroscientific Manual of Love
Homo: A Brief History of Consciousness
Neurosutra: The Abhijit Naskar Collection
Autobiography of God: Biopsy of A Cognitive Reality
Biopsy of Religions: Neuroanalysis towards Universal
Tolerance
Prescription: Treating India's Soul
What is Mind?
In Search of Divinity: Journey to The Kingdom of Conscience
Love, God & Neurons: Memoir of a scientist who found
himself by getting lost
The Islamophobic Civilization: Voyage of Acceptance
Neurons of Jesus: Mind of A Teacher, Spouse & Thinker
Neurons, Oxygen & Nanak
The Education Decree
Principia Humanitas
The Krishna Cancer
Rowdy Buddha: The First Sapiens
We Are All Black: A Treatise on Racism
The Bengal Tigress: A Treatise on Gender Equality
Either Civilized or Phobic: A Treatise on Homosexuality
Wise Mating: A Treatise on Monogamy
Illusion of Religion: A Treatise on Religious
Fundamentalism
The Film Testament
Human Making is Our Mission: A Treatise on Parenting
I Am The Thread: My Mission
7 Billion Gods: Humans Above All
Lord is My Sheep: Gospel of Human
Morality Absolute
A Push in Perception
Let The Poor Be Your God
Conscience over Nonsense
Saint of The Sapiens
Time to Save Medicine
Fabric of Humanity

Build Bridges not Walls: In the name of Americana
The Constitution of The United Peoples of Earth
Lives to Serve Before I Sleep
When Humans Unite: Making A World Without Borders
All For Acceptance
Monk Meets World
Mission Reality
Citizens of Peace: Beyond The Savagery of Sovereignty
Operation Justice: To Make A Society That Needs No Law
See No Gender
The Gospel of Technology
Every Generation Needs Caretakers: The Gospel of
Patriotism
Aşkanjali: The Sufi Sermon
Mad About Humans: World Maker's Almanac
Revolution Indomable
When Call The People: My World My Responsibility
No Foreigner Only Family
Hurricane Humans: Give me accountability, I'll give you
peace
Ain't Enough to Look Human
Servitude is Sanctitude

DEDICATION

This book is dedicated to Benjamin Franklin

CONTENTS

1. Sonnet of Meritocracy

Sonnet of Meritocracy

Where states dictate humanity,
Harmony remains an eternal fiction.
Diplomacy only divides people in secret,
And democracy sustains that foul friction.
Where the society is mesmerized by charm,
And politics is fueled by populism.
Values and character exist as theories,
As matter of talks, not as alive aphorism.
Under the sectarian watch of states,
Inclusion and acceptance turn to dust.
In an attempt to sustain sovereignty,
Humanity of the humans gets all lost.
Electing authorities on whim is only poker,
Without merit as core, democracy is
peacebreaker.

2. When A Human is Born

It's not enough to have only doctors without borders - the world needs scientists without borders - it needs artists without borders - it needs teachers without borders - it needs engineers without borders - in short, the world needs humans without borders. These humans won't be merely advocates of harmony, they'll be the very embodiment of harmony.

I am no advocate for harmony, I am the embodiment of harmony - I am what harmony looks like - I am the living proof of harmony. The whole world came together, only then Naskar came to life. Therefore I make this decree here and now - no nation, culture or religion is ever to proclaim exclusive ownership of my work - I belong to the whole of humankind, not to any single tribe.

The idea called Naskar was born by the Hooghly river, nourished by the Bosphorus and finally recognized and spread across the world from, next to the Hudson. That's why I have never felt belonging to any one place. But mark you, I am not saying that I have felt out of place, for places are myth, only people exist.

Wherever there are people, that's where I belong - today it's earth, tomorrow it's the moon, the day after mars and onwards. My body will be gone, but I won't, so long as there is even one human left to think of others before they think of themselves. These are the humans without borders.

Once you lose the borders, you'll find the world. Once you lose everything, you'll find yourself. Borders are to exist as a societal paradigm, they must not hold any emotional grip over the people. To put it simply, you may live with borders, but don't live in them, that is, let the borders be outside, not inside. Don't let them come into your mind no matter how much your state and media condition you to do so.

3. Let The Borders be Outside

I live on earth, not in any nation. Anybody who says, Naskar was born in this nation or that nation, hasn't understood a single word of my work. I have said many a times that, every nation is my nation, every religion is my religion, every culture is my culture.

Now here you may wonder, what does my identity has to do with you or even with democracy for that matter? And the answer is - everything - for my identity is not only my identity, it's your identity, it's the identity of our entire species. I and you are not separate - I repeat - I and you are not separate - you and others are not separate - we all are one identity – qualities belonging to one human, also belong to all humans.

At first there were tribes, then as our minds began to expand, the size of our tribes also began to expand, and then eventually we had nations. However, the dynamics between nations hasn't changed much from that of the dynamics between tribes in our old days. We still keep fighting the same old tribal battle, but with modern weapons and strategies - the means of the fight may have changed, but the fight itself remains the same. And some may turn their back on this fact, but that doesn't make the fact disappear.

Let me elaborate. Have you ever thought, why is it that whenever there is tension at the border, people of each nation are made to believe, primarily by their government, armed forces and media, that it's the fault of the neighboring nation - they are made to believe that their neighbor is always the aggressor - the Indian people are made to believe that China or Pakistan is the aggressor, the Azerbaijani people are made to believe that Armenia is the aggressor - the Bulgarian people are made to believe that Turkey is the aggressor - and so on. And not a single citizen questions this conviction, out of their primitive, stone-age tenets of nationalism.

Not a single nation on this planet has ever, till now, fully, unconditionally, uncompromisably devoted itself to the course of international harmony. Each state wants its people to feel, think and behave as loyal subjects in the best interest of their own nation over that of the neighboring nation, over that of the world. When will this nationalist barbarism end? When will this insane savagery end?

Raising fingers at each other will leave everyone without hands. Don't raise fingers, raise your conscience. And once you actually raise your conscience, you'll discover that most actions of the so-called state are never meant for peace on earth, they are meant for the exclusive security of their own nation over that of others.

But here's the point, till the people of a nation actually elevate their own conscience, there will never be peace, for no state will ever pay attention to the benefit of the neighboring nation over that of their own - an individual leader may, but states won't. States will always be invested exclusively in the benefit of one specific nation over that of others - they will always be invested exclusively in the security of one specific nation over the peace of the planet. This way, states are merely glorified tribal authorities, who are incapable of ensuring peace and progress in our world.

4. What States Care About

The fact that we were able to expand our sense of community from small tribes to much larger nations, makes it evident that if we have the genuine desire to build a united world, we can do so. It's not going to be easy, but, no great deed is ever easy, nevertheless it's necessary.

So how do we start - where do we even begin? And the answer is, ourselves. As long as you live as sheep, states will always have you do whatever they want, often at the price of world peace - so long as you keep sleeping, states will make you believe whatever they want. Till you wake up and demand peace for the world, no government will give a damn about peace on earth, they'll only pretend that they do.

Governments don't care about peace, governments only care about sovereignty - they only care about control - control of the people, control of the resources and control of the soil. Individuals may care for the world, but governments do not. Now here we must ask the question - why? To answer this, we must understand what government is. In ideological theory, government is an entire population, but in actual practice, government is only a bunch of people deciding the fate of an entire population.

Now here I am not saying that it would be better if there were no government to run a nation, although that should be the goal of a civilized society - but my question is, who are these people who make all the decisions for the population - what are their qualifications - what training do they have - and the answer is none - they are just random people chosen by the population on sheer appeal.

You feel anxious when being treated by a medical student who is yet to complete their training, but when it comes to the treatment of your nation, you have no trouble choosing any tom, dick and trump and let them do whatever they wish, while you watch from the sidelines as if you are watching an exciting baseball game. And you most proudly call this democracy. What an utter waste of brain power!

5. Humanizing Democracy
(A Sonnet)

Humanizing Democracy
(A Sonnet)

Dictatorship is rule of the cunning,
Democracy is rule of the halfwits.
Both are quite degrading for society,
Cause neither of them is born of merits.
Progress requires practice of reason,
Immersed in a whole lot of love.
But when the people prefer indifference,
Society regresses down the savage curve.
Character is the foundation of civilization,
Yet that character is taken for granted.
All talk and no walk has made us shallow,
Separatism has made our soul tainted.
So it's time we feed values into democracy,
While abolishing all populist fallacy.

6. Requirements of Democracy

Democracy can lift a nation only if the people are mature enough to understand the accountability of having a democracy. It's not enough to have democracy, you must practice the requirements of democracy. And the requirements of democracy are accountability and reason. Democracy without accountability leads only to death and destruction both in the nation and in the world.

And who's going to take responsibility for that death and destruction - nobody, cause every state will be busy raising fingers at each other. And if nobody is accountable then who's going to ensure justice - nobody - for there'll be no justice. In a world where indifference is the cornerstone of democracy, justice remains as a mere phantom.

No congress, no parliament, no law enforcement is going to ensure justice in the society, people must ensure their own justice, by empowering the righteous and the humane, and obliterating the atrocious and the savage from their authoritative position. Justice never comes softly, justice comes boldly. And more importantly, justice is not given, justice is to be taken.

Justice is not the exclusive responsibility of the law and the government, it is the responsibility of each human being on earth who has a beating heart and a thinking brain ("beating heart" refers to human emotions, not the organic heart, for the organic heart only pumps blood, it doesn't hold emotions, the brain does). In fact, government entrusts the law with the task of ensuring order and justice in the society, because the general population are not mature and civilized enough to comprehend even the meaning of justice and order.

A truly civilized society has no use of law and government, it's only an uncivilized society that needs them. Once we are truly civilized, there will be no law and government – crime will be treated by medicine and society will be run by similar distinct autonomous departments founded upon merit.

There will be no political authority - there will be no legal authority - there'll be no state authority. Distinct autonomous departments will handle distinct matters of the society. And the mutual exchange of these departments will keep them properly functional in the society, and in the event of a severe criminal offence, medical experts will handle the matter, just as they do today when there is a virus outbreak.

7. Next Step for Democracy

Liberty is only liberty when you are your own authority, but at the same time, when you start abusing that liberty and become a liability to the society, it no longer is liberty (considering it to be exclusively a human thing), but mere savagery, and savagery should either be cast back into the jungle or be treated with proper medical care till all the savage tenets are no longer dominant.

However, what I must mention is that, I am not talking about some utopian future where everything will be perfect and society will be flawless, for a flawless society is a mythical society. What I am proposing is a future for your children where they will be able to spread their wings without the fear of being persecuted or laughed at. And a democratic society, as we consider democracy today, will never be truly free from persecutions.

If you want to make a society free from persecutions, you must learn to step outside of democracy. And it's not like something like this hasn't happened before. Once dictators and kings ruled the world, then we started to understand the fallacy of such a societal structure, so we stepped outside of dictatorship and monarchy, and built a new and more civilized world with democracy.

And now the time has come again to take a similar decision, for democracy may have been a better alternative to dictatorship and monarchy at the time, but it no longer is compatible with a developing and globalizing world. Therefore, it's time to scrap democracy and build the new world with meritocracy, where merits and values will dictate affairs of society, not mere charm and charisma.

In such a society, people of specific skillsets and expertise will be placed in fields where they are most needed. Let me give you a very simple example. In such a society a janitor may be made the person in charge of keeping the society clean and sanitized, but they won't be placed in charge of the society's finances, likewise, an economist may be placed in charge of the society's finances, but not in charge of keeping the society clean and sanitized. In such a society nobody will be insignificant for everybody will have their role to play.

8. Principles of Meritocracy

Democracy won't do much good for peace and progress in the world, only meritocracy will. And we can take the revolutionary leap from democracy to meritocracy right now - dissolve the government and all political offices, and keep the departments that actually run a nation anyways.

Once that's done, that is, once the various departments or sectors of society, such as health, education, legal, finance, transport and so on, are freed from political authority and control, then in the next step of reform, we'll have to work on the departments themselves to elevate them into a truly civilized state. But again, the very first step of reforming democracy into meritocracy is to demolish the very concept of politics and politician. Without doing that we cannot achieve much civilized reform. Without abolishing politics we cannot build a civilized world.

Now here we have primarily two obstacles, the first one is of course demolishing politics, which we'll address in a little while, for it demands far more contemplation, perseverance and determination, than the next one, which is reforming the departments themselves, once we have eliminated all traces of politics.

In the world we live in, or I should say in the democracy we live in, politicians without any expertise in any specific field ultimately decide the fate of the sectors of a nation, thus deciding the fate of the people - it's like asking the blind to guide the way. So, once we have abolished politics, one specific department will have to be raised consisting experts in social sciences, who will take essential decisions on whether and how to improve an existing department or to make it a part of another one, for example, as I mentioned earlier, crime will ultimate fall under the turf of medicine, that is, health department.

Capital punishment and imprisonment will be abolished and in their place there will be rehabilitation. Prisons will be replaced with rehabilitation centers where those found guilty of a crime will be treated by doctors. Court system will be abolished including the very profession of lawyers and in its place there'll be ethics council, which will consist of equal number of experts from all existing departments.

People can submit their grievances to the ethics council, and those grievances will be handled by distinct experts of the council based on the nature of the grievance. In the investigation of each case the ethics council experts will be aided by a medical expert, to make sure that the case doesn't involve any kind of pathology. In short, it'll be the responsibility of the ethics council to ensure justice in the society.

And of course, no human is incorruptible, including those working in specific departments of the society, so like monthly physical checkup there'll be monthly psych evaluation, which will include evaluation of primitive tenets. And if a person shows signs of greed, bigotry, fundamentalism, misogyny, homophobia or any such primitive behavior, they'll be enlisted for rehabilitation.

Instead of running a nation like a political circus by brainless politicians (not all politicians are brainless), a nation should be run like a kindergarten where the teachers would be beings of character and expertise (both). And if meritocracy is the kindergarten then right now we are in the womb. So, you can imagine how long a journey it is till we even begin to call ourselves adults. Yet that's what being sapiens means, to start the journey of a thousand centuries with one step, and that one step towards a distant civilized society starts with the abolition of political positions.

9. Who Actually Run A Nation

The first principle of social development is, authority doesn't solve a problem, expertise guided by character does. So, if you leave the issues of the world to be solved by individuals who have no expertise in those specific issues, then you yourself are signing the death sentence for your society - having done that, you have no right to shout and rally for justice.

First learn to recognize the root of the problem - then think and talk about solution. Right now you think about the solution to the social issues exactly the way the authorities of your society want you to think - and they let you do so, because they know that it won't even move a hair from their head.

So forget the solutions for a while, and think what the problem is. The problem is not that the politicians are corrupt or that the cops are corrupt or that the lawyers are corrupt, the real problem is that you yourself have allowed a paradigm which facilitates such corruption - so if you want to end the corruption, you have to end the very paradigm that sustains it - in short, you have to end democracy.

Hence comes the first obstacle that I mentioned earlier - the obstacle of the first leap from meritocracy to democracy, that is, the abolition of political positions. Now do not panic, for it may sound earth-shaking at the moment, but once you go deeper into the matter you'd start to feel otherwise. Let me give you an example. When you are sick, you go to the doctor, the doctor based on his or her years of rigorous medical training and expertise diagnoses your problem and provides you the proper treatment - they don't ask the local politician what treatment they should give you.

In the same way, when you send your kid off to school, the teacher doesn't ask the local politician how to teach - then when you catch the bus, the bus driver doesn't ask the local politician how to drive or which route to take. In these practical circumstances of life, you rely on the expertise of individuals anyways - you rely on their merit - which means your life is practical moving forward through meritocracy-society is moving forward through meritocracy.

Thus, all the real responsibility is carried by meritocracy, while know-nothing politicians take credit for it through the illusive democracy that you yourself have erected for them. All I am asking is that you destroy that illusion of democracy and simply acknowledge the involvement and contributions of the people who actually run a nation anyways, while the politicians take all the glory without any of the liability.

10. The First Step of Meritocracy

Recognize in your heart who actually run a society - accept it with every breath - only then can the path manifest in front of your eyes. Let me put it into perspective for the ease of recognition - a janitor does more for the society than a politician - a doctor does more for the society than a politician - a teacher does more for the society than a politician - a construction worker does more for the society than a politician.

How is this meritocracy one may wonder, so let me make it clear. The cleanliness of your neighborhood street depends on the merit of a janitor - the education of your child depends on a teacher - the timely completion of a building depends on a construction worker and so on. And that my friend is meritocracy in action. Meritocracy is at work in every aspect of your life, it just didn't dawn on you till now. Think of meritocracy as the ghost writer and democracy the face. But this can't continue, for those know-nothing politicians have done enough damage already.

However, not much will change in your practical life, once we move from democracy to meritocracy – the change that will occur is that the concern, will and activities surrounding human welfare in the human society will increase exponentially. You'll continue living your life the way you are living now, all that'll change is that power will be taken out of the hands of the politicians and given to the people. And that's called civilization.

11. Empowering Good Politicians

Now, before we continue any further, I must make something very clear. Not all those who are in politics are there to serve the interest of themselves, a few, that is, a rare few individuals often become involved in the so-called politics who have at the core of their being the burning desire to serve the people, and I will continue to stand by such individuals so long as I live, but at the same time my work also demands that I prepare the road to a better and less animal future, and to do that, we cannot simply hope and wait for some rare gold-hearted individuals to come in politics once in a while and take our society ahead.

We must aim towards building a society that eliminates the very possibility of any corrupt or unfit person coming to power. This is not an easy task at all, and nor is it black and white - it requires a lot of thinking, determination and action from each and every capable member of the society.

Our aim should be to eliminate politics altogether, but in the meantime, we must continue to humanize the democracy of today by empowering the good politicians and methodically placing political power only in the hands of the capable through proper training and licensing, like in medical practice, and not through random selection and election of candidates, (as I have depicted thoroughly in "The Constitution of The United Peoples of Earth", which can be considered the prequel to this book) while preparing ourselves to take charge of our society in the land beyond politics.

In such a civilized society free from politics, lives of the people should be guided by the people themselves - but this specific part is extremely grey, so let's investigate slower and deeper. What does it mean for the people to guide their own lives – it means that distinct affairs of a society of humans will be guided the humans based on their merit in those affairs - medical professionals will decide matters of healthcare - teachers and experts in pedagogy will decide matters of education and so on.

12. Till We Abolish Politics

The only way we can build a truly civilized and peaceful world is if we get rid of politics altogether, but till we can accomplish that, we must, not should, but must bring training and licensing into politics, like we have in medicine, or else humankind will continue to suffer from civil wars and international conflicts.

No people in the world want war, they only want a happy and healthy future for their family, it's the state that fills them up with hate against the neighbor in the name of patriotism. Peace is a state of mind, but in a world where the state controls the mind, peace remains an inconvenience. If you want peace in the world, shut your ears to authority and open your mind to reason and humanity.

Remember, the professionals may be skilled at doing their work, but not politicians, for politics is not a profession, it's a game of poker, in which people are not the player, but merely the stakes, and as such all you can do is to hope that you get lucky by being played by a benevolent politician.

Even a doctor has to go through almost a decade of rigorous training to take care of people's health, and as for a politician who is to take care of the very lives of the people, there is no training! What kind of a deplorable stupidity is this? And we glorify this stupidity with the title of democracy. And with this stupidity we wish there to be inclusion - with this stupidity we wish there to be harmony - with this stupidity we wish there to be equality and justice.

We may wish all we want, but it won't happen in a million years. We must recognize our stupidity - we must recognize our errors - we must recognize the flaws in the societal paradigm that we live in, only then can we step forward in a civilized direction.

13. In Merit We Ought to Trust

You may think that just because you have wifi, netflix and mcdonalds, the work to build a civilized society is done, but let me tell you this, the work is far from done. We have merely managed to invent the tools to speed up the work, but the work itself is yet to be finished. So, sleep not, slacken not. Remember, sleep of conscience, awakening of prejudice.

And indeed that conscience appears to be asleep in most of humanity, or else governments across the world wouldn't be able to poison people against people. Governments continue to poison the minds of the people with the mentality of war instead of organizing peace - and it's because we let the governments do so - we let the states dictate the paradigm of our society. But it's time we break this savage habit of ours - the habit to delegate the affairs of our life to a handful few with no proper education and training in peace and progress.

No paradigm is stronger than human determination - if you are determined, you can breathe life even into a barren desert - breaking and reforming a paradigm is merely child's play for you - for you as in the human you, that is, for the being who has awakened from the popular sleep of indifference and prejudice. As long as you are asleep, even the dumbest of governments will control your every move. Wake up and all governments will collapse. If you must trust, trust people, not paradigms.

In a civilized society, people should trust people, not paradigms - in a civilized society people should trust expertise, not charm - in a civilized society people should trust character, not charisma. A society built upon charisma is destined for ruin.

People like to shout a statement which was first voiced by our beloved Honest Abe - democracy is a rule of the people, for the people and by the people. Today this statement is merely a tool in the hands of new-age dictators, whom you call leaders. Except for the times when the society has been guided by the hands of actual conscientious characters, democracy has rarely been a rule of the people, for the people and by the people - in practice, democracy is a rule of the politicians, for the politicians and by the politicians. And unless we change that, no two nations will live in peace and harmony for long.

To reform democracy into an actual rule of the people, we must abolish all traces of politics, and place the power - no "power" is not the right word here - we must place our trust in the hands of the capable, in the hands of the skilled, in the hands of the conscientious - in short, we must take back all trust from the hands of politicians and place them in the hands of those with merit and expertise in various aspects of life.

In fact, meritocracy is not at all different or separate from democracy - meritocracy is the true democracy, where the society is actually taken forward by the people, literally, with skill and character. To put it simply, meritocracy is the fulfillment of democracy, not the destruction of it.

14. Building A Stateless Society

The problem is, the world has become so dependent upon the disfigured shape of democracy, that it can barely comprehend the meaning of it or more importantly the implications of it. Democracy means accountability, but to the people, it's quite the opposite - to the people democracy means getting rid of all accountability by leaving it to someone else. With such savage democracy society can only move backwards, not forward.

We cannot create a truly democratic society till we create a stateless society. Resources of the society must be distributed among the people according to need, yet in today's so-called democracy resources are distributed according to greed, and the situation will only worsen with time till we stop delegating the affairs of our life to random individuals of charm and popularity. Democracy driven by populism leads to a savage, superstitious and divided society, not a civilized, thinking and united one.

And once the people recognize this simple fact, democracy will turn into meritocracy in no time. Yet, sometimes the simplest fact is too complex for the people to understand, and even when they do pretend to understand, they fail to practice it in real life, for real understanding requires accountability, whereas the masses are keen on having liberty without accountability.

Nevertheless, if we can bring people together under the banner of nation, we can also bring people together under the banner of humanity, it's only a matter of time and perseverance. It won't happen in my lifetime - it won't happen in your lifetime - it won't even happen in the lifetime of your children, but we can either be active builders of that humane future or insignificant animals stuck in the primitive past.

15. No Society is Born Humane

No society is born humane (not yet, evolutionarily speaking), it has to be made humane. No society is born just, it has to be made just. No society is born great, it must be made great, and for that each human much contribute at the fullest of their capacity.

Nobody is born with a purpose, for all that "destined to do this and that" thing is merely superstitious nonsense which people tell themselves to ease the anxiety of the unknown - the fact of the matter is, when we are born, we are no different from any other animal on earth, and as we grow up, we must discover a purpose for ourselves, only then can we be called higher than the animals.

As I have said a few times before, without purpose we are just good-looking animals. Nobody is destined to do anything - and nobody is not destined to anything either, it's our own determination and understanding that endow us with our own purpose, and once endowed with a purpose, it's our unwillingness to give up on that purpose that makes us human.

Work my brave sisters and brothers for a just and humane society. We shall see the light soon.

Be brave - be brave - person dies but once - be brave and work on. Ever since I started my work of world building I haven't taken a single day of rest - absolute, uncorrupted devotion to the cause, that's the only road to success.

I don't ask you to live by my words, I ask you to die for your purpose - whatever that purpose may be - whatever that cause may be. If you are not ready to die for a purpose, you are not ready to live. Die for a purpose or live for nothing. Life without purpose is a life wasted. It's our purpose that makes us human, not our appearance. In appearance everybody looks human, but that says nothing about the humanity of that creature - in action that creature may be the most savage animal in the world.

16. Liberating
An Imprisoned Society

Deeds are the measure of humanity, not looks. Those who pay attention to looks, know nothing of humanity and those who pay attention to humanity, care nothing about looks. We live in a world where nationality is given importance, race is given importance, religion is given importance, political affiliation is given importance, gender and sexuality are given importance – way above the importance of humanity.

I am pain-stricken to say, in today's society the very humanity of a person is determined based on their nationality, race, religion, political affiliation, gender, sexuality and so on - as if, humanity is so puny that it could be packaged and labeled with the stale identities of society! Humanity is far too grand to be locked up in the prison of tribalism. Yet, we have been attempting to do exactly the same since we learnt to live apart from the animals - and till we free humanity from that prison, no paradigm can ensure health, sanity and serenity in the society.

Some may shout, socialism will make us free - others may shout, capitalism will take us forward - but all this shouting only creates noise, not actual solutions to the problems that haunt our society. Theories are plenty, ideologies are plenty, and though they are all presented as ideal, when they are put to practice in the real world, their shortfalls begin to show up and one system's shortfalls become the focus of criticism for the advocates of other systems.

The point is, you don't have to be acquainted with all the philosophical and political ideologies to build a just society - you just need to feel responsible for the society - you just need to have the genuine will to do good for your society - that very responsibility when accompanied by reason will give rise to all the understanding that you'd need to serve the best interest of the society.

Till this day there are many political and philosophical terminologies that I do not know the meaning of, yet that doesn't bother me the least, for the true essence of virtues lies in deeds, not in pompous terminologies. Let people label your work if they so wish - you just keep doing your work.

That is why I prefer not to use pompous philosophical and political terminologies unless absolutely necessary. I use simple words to voice my simple ideas. The world is already filled with fancy words and concepts, yet they haven't made the world any more peaceful and humane.

It is this simple, terminologies and ideologies may attempt to determine and define the nature and characteristics of humanity, but they are bound to fail, for humanity is beyond all ideologies – it is beyond all paradigms – it is beyond the petty compartmental mentality of the tribal creatures who like to call themselves humans - and since there is no other creature to question their conviction, they most proudly continue to call themselves humans without the slightest bit of societal accountability that is required of a true human.

17. No Place for Walls

They fight over ideologies - they fight over concepts and images - they concoct all sorts of walls in their head, all of which are illusive, then they fight over the supremacy of one wall over the other. A human who is truly human won't be able to live within walls, they wouldn't be able to breathe, only the primitives feel secure behind walls.

To instill real peace in the world, we must first take down the walls, after that we can take steps for further progress. No lasting progress can be ensured so long as the common human mind is stuck behind walls. Take down the walls that have torn your own mind into pieces and acceptance will pour out of your mind into the world on its own. So long as there is obstruction in the path of a river, it cannot flow, but remove the obstruction and the river continues to flow on its own, the same is with acceptance - the same is with harmony - the same is with peace.

Sisters and brothers of my world, I do not believe in universal acceptance, for I am the very embodiment of universal acceptance. The river doesn't believe in the life-giving powers of its water - the sun doesn't believe in the warmth-giving powers of its rays - the wind doesn't believe in the soothing powers of its breeze. Belief implies an absence of proof, but acceptance is beyond proof. You do not believe that you need oxygen to live, likewise, you do not believe in universal acceptance, for without it, the very fabric of civilization will wither. Universal acceptance is the oxygen for civilization - it is the lifeblood of a civilized society.

To build a civilization is not as simple as building a rocket or a car. It requires us to stand up to our own inner evil, but here we must be very clear about the term evil. The term evil simply refers to the primitive aspects of human nature - in short it refers to the animal side of a living human. Once we tame our inner beast, shaping the world outside will be child's play. Once we reform the universe inside, our each footstep will trigger a cascade of reform in the universe outside.

18. All Reform Starts With You

To reform the society, you must reform the self first. All reformation has its origin in the self. Without the reformation of the self, no reformation of the outside world can last long. Therefore, reformation of the self first, then the society. Yet, we've built our world exactly in the opposite direction, that's why it's still infested with disparities, discrimination and destitution despite all our scientific and technological achievements.

However, I am not undermining the external advancements that we have made, but imagine a time when the external world is highly sophisticated yet the internal world of the people is absolutely devastated - and that's the direction in which we've been moving. And if we don't do anything about it right now, later it'll be too late, just like if we don't take action to tackle climate change right now, later it'll be too late.

We can continue with our external development as we have been carrying out till now, but at the same time we must engage equally, if not more, in our internal development, without which all the external achievements in the world won't be able to instill sanity, serenity and unity in life and society.

Evolutionarily speaking, no society is born to live in peace, they are all born to survive in a wild environment at all costs, because millions of years of existence in the wild has conditioned our psyche in that way. If we want to change that, we have to take the conscious and willful decision to free ourselves from the clutches of mother nature's monstrosity that lurks in the dark corners of our mind. And once we do that, only then the society will be free from the clutches of its inherent darkness. The darkness will still be there mark you, but it won't be as dominant as today.

19. The Meaning of Merit

Our elevation into light from darkness won't be easy, at times weakness will grab you by the throat, but it is imperative that you do not submit to complacency. Even the strongest of sages turns weak at times. Weakness is not the problem, submission to weakness is. Accept weakness as part of life, but never submit to it.

Now here some may wonder - what's the difference between accepting weakness and submitting to weakness? And the answer is quite simple and straightforward. Submitting to weakness means giving the control of your life to that weakness, whereas accepting weakness means working through the weakness without either resenting it or exaggerating it.

There should be one ultimate goal in front of your eyes - to alleviate the darkness from the world. And it doesn't happen by delegating all accountability of the world to a bunch of know-it-alls. You must take the responsibility on your own shoulders, based on your own ability and strongholds. You don't need to start with the problems of the world, start with the problems of your neighborhood.

Don't stand by waiting for some politician to come and solve the problems of your neighborhood, gather people with different expertise from your neighborhood and work according to the instructions of those whose expertise relates most to the problems. Rely on merit to solve the problems of your society, not on the pity of politicians.

However, we must first understand what merit is. Merit is not merely skill or expertise, it is much more than that. Merit is expertise guided by character. Here the term expertise is quite simple and straightforward, but the term character is where the true beauty of merit lies. Character is what guides expertise in the right direction. Without the guidance of a well-built character, expertise alone cannot keep the individual and the society in the course of humanity.

Character is not one quality of a human. It's the essence of humanity - it's the very foundation of a civilized human psyche. Character means everything that is human about you. And such a grand meaning cannot be depicted with a few words, yet let's try to paint a picture of it with the striking tenets that compose a person's character.

Character means a sense of community - character means a desire for learning and growth - character means the guts to admit and mend one's own errors and shortcomings - character means the yearning for assimilation. Where there is character, there is growth and harmony - no character, no growth – no character, no harmony. Hence a truly civilized society is built upon the edifice of character. And excellence is the most powerful tool in the hands of a well-built character.

That my friend is what meritocracy is about, it's about building a society which is shaped by excellence and guided by character. In such a society, there is no place for prejudice, there is no place of sectarianism, there is no place for primitive tribalism. In such a society all delusions of separatism would collapse into dust. In such a society each human would be omnipresent, for all humans will see the reflection of themselves in each other. I am here and I am there, the distance is only a foul delusion - the root of all separation. Destroy the delusion from the soil of your psyche and all will be one.

20. Either Divisive or Civilized

Today's so-called democratic world is founded upon divisiveness, for the main ingredient of this democracy is neither reason nor compassion, but extremism, be it nationalist extremism or religious extremism. And these qualities may have served us well in the jungle but they have no healthy role to play in a civilized society.

In short, to build a civilized world all nationalism and religious extremism must be discarded at once. Nations are myths, the sooner you realize this, the sooner you can be called responsible parents of your children, because by entertaining the savage concepts of nations and borders and cultural supremacy, you yourself are casting your children into a life of discrimination, prejudice and phobia. If you do not want that, then you must change - you must change from an animal into a human. We are all born animals, but at some point we must turn ourselves into humans, and that requires discarding of all tribalism.

And you cannot do that so long as you keep relying on shallow authorities whose very existence is founded upon that tribalism. But mark you, I am not in any way advocating for mere rebellion against the state or some cheap mindless anarchy, what I am asking of you is that you be accountable of your society and take charge of the societal matters in which you have an expertise. Remember, everyone has some sort of expertise in something, but if you still do not know what your expertise is, then empower the expertise of those around and solve the problems of your society guided by them.

If the authorities of society are not in the course of reason and assimilation then rejecting such authorities and replacing them with a logical and humane alternative is not anarchy, it's the existential duty of every thinking and feeling human. But I repeat, rejecting the authorities is not enough, if you do not have an actual alternative to replace those authorities with. The rejecting and replacing do not take place separately, they must take place simultaneously - as a matter of fact, the act of replacing itself is the best rejection. So start thinking how you can make your society better - then act on that thought, with or without the support of the state.

21. Laying The Foundation of Meritocracy

States have such power over people because people are complacent. Stop being complacent, and the very shape of the state will be reformed. In fact, the state itself will be compelled to replace its political figureheads with actual individuals of merit if the people had the guts to stand up and demand it. But since the people don't care, state doesn't care either. And it continues to drive the society down the path of regress with a democracy filled with meritless idiots, instead of asking for guidance from those with merit.

Democracy can cause either regress or progress depending on the character of the people. Sleeping masses make a regressive democracy, whereas thinking masses make a progressive democracy. Parties exist because people allow it - borders exist because people allow it - wars exist because people allow it. But if you make it a habit to resort to merit instead of charisma for the solutions to the problems of your society, the very foundation of today's democracy would be renovated into a meritocratic one without any further strategic efforts.

You change, you the individual - change your daily habits - change your way of life - and the society is bound to change. It's not rocket science, it's much simpler than that, yet it's the most difficult task in the world, a thousand times more difficult than building a rocket, nevertheless all it takes is the genuine desire in a handful of individuals to step up and act.

Some people build cars, some rockets, I build humans. Building a rocket is complex yet easy, whereas building a civilized society is simple yet difficult. And to build a civilized society is no work of the weak-hearted or the prejudiced, it's the work of the living Gods, it's the work of humans without borders. And to build these humans is the work of my life. But how do I do that? Do I do it as a teacher - no, for the society has only raised high walls of differentiation around the greatest teachers of history - so, I do it, not as a teacher, but simply as an example - I simply be the human that I desire to wake up in you.

I am a human without borders, and should you wish to be one as well, never ever make the mistake of taking me for a teacher, instead let's walk together - let's walk together in the course of world building - let's walk together in the course of reason - let's walk together in the course of assimilation. Let's admit that we all are idiots, and start working from there, so that we can build a world that is less of an idiot, for the first step of progress is the acknowledgement of ignorance. Only when you accept that you do not know, will you feel the urge to learn and only when you learn, can you grow as an individual - and only when you grow as an individual, we'll grow as a society.

Remember, meritocracy is not given, it is to be built upon the blood and sweat of every being of conscience and character - meritocracy is to be built upon the accountability of every thinking and feeling human. Civilization will not magically arrive from somewhere, it's already inside you - recognize it, realize it and bring it out through action. A whole humane world is dancing inside your heart, let every molecule in your body resonate with its rhythm and once you do, the world outside will start dancing in the steps of humaneness. Your heart holds the power to build a thousand civilizations, won't you build just one my friend!

22.Individuals Die, Not Ideas

I searched heaven and earth for a gift for my beloved - my humanity, I found nothing suitable, so I place the offering of my life at your feet. I am not your teacher, I am not your guide, I am not your savior, I am but a humble human high on love for you.

Some may come around peddling my work as instruction manuals, but listen not to those divisive barbarians. My work is not some instruction manual of life, nor does it consist of any divine revelation of some so-called truth. I am your lover, and all I do is pour my love into letters so that you may look straight into my soul across space and time.

My books are not books but letters to every thinking and feeling human across time, the purpose of which is to galvanize the human in you to action. The purpose of my life is to make reformers out of every conscientious human, and love is the greatest force of reformation there is - the purpose of my life is to make humanitarians out of every thinking human by pouring all my love into their existence - the purpose of my life is to make immortal Gods out of every mortal human.

I am no writer on revolution and reform, I am the very language of revolution and reform - I am no writer on justice and equality, I am the very language of justice and equality - I am no writer on acceptance and harmony, I am the very language of acceptance and harmony. And my story is not my story, but the story of every single thinking and feeling human on earth.

I am nameless, I am timeless, I am deathless, for I am the indestructible force of humanhood, and one biological vessel isn't enough for the fulfillment of this force, it'll continue to fasten onto every potential vessel through time till all traces of divisiveness and superstition are abolished from the world.

I am not talking about reincarnation mark you. Reincarnation is but a supernatural invention by the savage minds of yesterday in an attempt to take comfort in an imaginary endlessness of life. Bold and humanizing ideas need no supernatural nonsense to manifest in the world, they always manage to find mortal vessels to exist across time. Individuals die, not ideas.

All it takes is one person in every hundred years or so to be possessed with a revolutionary idea, and that neurochemical madness in one brain keeps the torch of humaneness burning in the heart of humanity for at least a few centuries. Thus the world never runs out of ideas to be vitalized by in the attempts to become more human and less animal.

These ideas are the stepping stones of progress. And they'll continue to humanize the world so long as there is a single human left on earth. I can tell you this, one day all walls of religion, nation and culture will vanish and all that will remain is a simple sense of universal humanity. In that time and age, human actions will be guided by observation and compassion and not by imagination and insecurity.

23. Living Proof of The Future

The work for the future without walls must begin today. I exist as a living proof of that future, but it's not enough, every single thinking and feeling human must become a living proof of that future, for only then can the walls that divide humanity vanish from the face of earth.

You may think you are too little and insignificant to achieve such a grand task, but look at the bees - one little bee can make a giant human jump up and down in agony with its almost invisible sting and it can also bestow health upon a person with its sweet, nourishing nectar. Appearance means nothing, for potential is immeasurable. You don't need sophisticated tools and institutions to change the world, all the tools that you need are already inside you.

For example, I use words to change the world, because guns are outdated. If guns could instill peace in the world, the world would have turned peaceful long ago. Guns will never ensure security and serenity, so put down your guns for good and sit down to talk. Telling people mere stories of peace won't make peace, they must feel the peace, and for that, you must feel the peace - you must become peace.

You must become the flame of peace so that the people around can actually feel your warmth. You must become whatever you want your society to be. Don't just shout for harmony, be the harmony for humanity - be the inclusion incarnate to humanity - be the assimilation incarnate to humanity.

Wake up and soar my centurions - the unification and ascension of our humankind are in your hands now. Bother not with those who keep sleeping despite your repeated calls - move ahead with an emboldened chest and let all obstructions turn to dust as they collide with your gargantuan determination. There is no grand, divine plan behind your existence, you need to make and work the plan yourself.

24. Ideas Over Paradigms

Find your path and walk on it till your last breath. The aim is to lift the world, and to achieve that try whatever works. Don't get too stuck on terms like democracy and meritocracy. Simply recognize your own merit and use it to lift your own community.

If you think you can lift your community as a teacher, be the best teacher you can - if you think you can do it as a scientist or philosopher, be the best scientist or philosopher you can - if you think you can do it as a cop, be the best cop you can - and if you think you can do it as a politician, say a president, be the best president you can.

It doesn't matter whether your intentions and chosen path to lift the world are compatible with some ideology and the constitution or not, for ideologies and constitutions are made to serve the people, not the other way around. So if a new, revolutionary idea rises which has the potential to benefit the world, then all constitutions, traditions and ideologies are to be amended to aid that idea, if they don't then the very progress of a nation will come to a halt.

For example, if an immigrant's daughter can become the vice-president of our United States, then the day is not far that even an immigrant can become the president - of course it'll require further amendments to the constitution, but that day our sweet land of liberty will truly be an advanced nation on earth. In fact, a nation can progress only if it adapts its societal paradigm with new, revolutionary ideas.

No constitution in the world is worth more than human life. So, anything that has the power to do good to life and society, it may be opposed by the paradigm at first, but no paradigm is strong enough to obstruct the path of an idea with the power to do good for long. Remember, strong ideas never give in to paradigms, it's the paradigms that must give in to ideas in an attempt to adapt to those ideas. So stand strong without bending as the living manifestation of an idea and all paradigms will bow before you.

25. Break, Don't Bend

They say if you don't bend, you break. I say it's better to break for a purpose than to bend for nothing. Discover your purpose, your idea and stick to it till the end. No matter the circumstances, never compromise your purpose - shatter to pieces for that purpose - become ashes for that purpose - but never, I repeat, never ever bend an inch.

We cannot create a world of character till there are humans with character. And it all starts with you. It only takes one generation of humans to break the chain of indifference and snobbery, and once you do that, progress and assimilation will pick up speed on their own. Forget what your parents and grandparents believed in or not believed in, they lived in a different time, and essentially in a different world - a tribal world - it's time that we grow out of the tribalism of our ancestors and start thinking in accordance with the new society - the global society. Tribal attitude won't work any more, because externally we have started to live in a non-tribal world, so it is imperative that we start living in a non-tribal world internally as well.

A united world starts with a human who is united and not divided inside. We have been divided for long - no more - no more - it is time - it is time to use our common sense and get rid of our divisions. You don't need to be a scientist to unite the world, common sense would suffice. Science reveals the details of nature, but to understand the most important truths of nature, common sense is enough. And till assimilation, inclusion and harmony become matters of common sense, no scientist, philosopher and preacher can bring people together. It's one thing to talk about harmony and completely another to actually feel that harmony in one's marrow.

Remember, the marrow of humans is the marrow of society - the backbone of humans is the backbone of society - hence, if your marrow is replete with segregation - if your backbone is made of tribalism, then no technology, no sociology, no ideology can sustain the integrity and sanity of our world. Inclusion in mind, inclusion in society - assimilation in mind, assimilation in society - ascension in mind, ascension in society.

So I repeat again something I've said countless times - wake up, start walking and stop not till the world is lifted. Everybody falls - make your fall spectacular and rise like a god, so that watching you even the voiceless regain their voice and the weak regain their strength.

BIBLIOGRAPHY

Archer M., (2000), Being Human: The Problem of Agency. Cambridge University Press.

Archer M., (2003), Structure, Agency and the Internal Conversation. Cambridge University Press.

Adolphs R (2003) Cognitive neuroscience of human social behaviour. Nature Rev Neurosci 4: 165–178.

Adolphs R, Tranel D, Damasio AR (2003) Dissociable neural systems for recognizing emotions. Brain Cogn 52: 61–69.

Afton, A. D. (1985). Forced copulation as a reproductive strategy of male lesser scaup: A field test of some predictions. - Behaviour 92, p. 146-167.

Allison T, Puce A, McCarthy G. (2000) Social perception from visual cues: role of the STS region. Trends Cogn Sci 4: 267–278.

Andresen, Jensine, and Robert Forman, eds. Cognitive Models and Spiritual Maps. Bowling Green, Ohio: Imprint Academic, 2000.

Ashbrook, James, and Carol Albright. The Humanizing Brain: Where Religion and Neuroscience Meet. Cleveland, OH: Pilgrim Press, 1997.

Azari, Nina, Janpeter Nickel, Gilbert Wunderlich, Michael Niedeggen, Harald Hefter, Lutz Tellmann, Hans Herzog, Petra Stoerig, Dieter Birnbacher, and Rudiger Seitz. "Neural Correlates of Religious Experience." European Journal of Neuroscience 13, no. 8 (2001)

Agar, N. (2004). Liberal eugenics: In defence of human enhancement. London: Blackwell Publishing.

Alteheld, N., Roessler, G., Vobig, M., & Walter, R. (2004). The retina implant new approach to a visual prosthesis. Biomedizinische Technik, 49(4), 99–103.

Antal, A., Nitsche, M. A., Kincses, T. Z., Kruse, W., Hoffmann, K. P., & Paulus, W. (2004a). Facilitation of visuo-motor learning by transcranial direct current stimulation of the motor and extrastriate visual areas in humans. European Journal of Neuroscience, 19(10), 2888–2892.

Bhat Z, Kumar, S, Bhat H (2015) In vitro meat production. Challenges and benefits over conventional meat production. J Sci Food Agric 14: 241–248

Bernstein R. J., (1967), John Dewey. New York: Washington Square Press.

Bernstein R.J., (1971), Praxis and Action: Contemporary Philosophies of Human Activity. Philadelphia: University of Pennsylvania Press.

Bernstein R.J., (1976), The Restructuring Social and Political Thought.

Bernstein R.J., (1983), Beyond Relativism and Objectivism: Science, Hermeneutics, and Praxis. Philadelphia: University of Pennsylvania Press.

Bernstein R.J., (1986), Philosophical Profiles. Philadelphia: University of Pennsylvania Press.

Bernstein R.J., (1991), New Constellation. Cambridge: MIT Press.

Barash, D. P. (1977). Sociobiology of rape in mallards (Anas platyrhynchos): Responses of the mated male. - Science 197, p. 788-789.

Berger, J. (1986). Wild horses of the great basin: Social competition and population size. - The University of Chicago Press, Chicago.

Birkhead, T. R., Johnson, S. D. & Nettleship, D. N. (1985). Extra-pair matings and mate guarding in the common murre Uria aalge. - Anim. Behav. 33, p. 608-619.

Beauregard, Mario, and Vincent Paquette. "Neural Correlates of a Mystical Experience in Carmelite Nuns." Neuroscience Letters 405, no. 3 (2006)

Benson, Herbert. Timeless Healing: The Power and Biology of Belief. New York: Scribner, 1996

Bogen, J.E.(1995a), 'On the neurophysiology of consciousness: Part I. An overview', Consciousness and Cognition, 4.

Bogen, J.E. (1995b), 'On the neurophysiology of consciousness: Part II. Constraining the semantic problem', Consciousness and Cognition, 4.

Bremner, J. D., R. Soufer, et al. (2001). "Gender differences in cognitive and neural correlates of remembrance of emotional words." Psychopharmacol Bull 35 (3).

Brothers, L. (2002). The social brain: A project for integrating primate behavior and neurophysiology in a new domain. In J. T. Cacioppo et al. (Eds.), Foundations in neuroscience. Cambridge, MA: MIT Press.

Buss, D. D. (2003). Evolutionary Psychology: The New Science of Mind, 2nd ed. New York: Allyn & Bacon.

Buss, D. M. (1989). "Conflict between the sexes: Strategic interference and the evocation of anger and upset." J Pers Soc Psychol 56 (5).

Buss, D. M. (1995). "Psychological sex differences. Origins through sexual selection." Am Psychol 50 (3).

Buss, D. M. (2002). "Review: Human Mate Guarding." Neuro Endocrinol Lett 23 (Suppl 4).

Buss, D. M., and D. P. Schmitt (1993). "Sexual strategies theory: An evolutionary perspective on human mating." Psychol Rev 100 (2).

Blakemore SJ, Decety J (2001) From the perception of action to the understanding of intention. Nature Rev Neurosci 2: 561.

Bruce C, Desimone R, Gross CG (1981) Visual properties of neurons in a polysensory area in superior temporal sulcus of the macaque. J Neurophysiol 46: 369–384.

Buccino G, Vogt S, Ritzl A, Fink GR, Zilles K, Freund HJ, Rizzolatti G (2004) Neural circuits underlying imitation of hand actions: an event related fMRI study. Neuron 42: 323–34.

Colapietro V., (1988), "Human Agency: The Habits of Our Being."

Southern Journal of Philosophy, XXVI, 2, pp. 153-68.

Colapietro V., (1992), "Purpose, Power, and Agency." The Monist, 75, 4 (October) pp. 423-44.

Colapietro V., (2003), "Signs and their vicissitudes: Meanings in excess of consciousness and functionality." Logica, Dialogica, Ideologica, a cure di Susan Petrilli e Patrizia Calefato (Milano: Mimesis), pp. 221-36.

Colapietro V., (2004a), "C. S. Peirce's Reclamation of Teleology." Nature in American Philosophy, ed. Jean De Groot (Washington, D.C.: Catholic University Press of America), pp. 88-108.

Colapietro V., (2004b), "Portrait of a Historicist: An Alternative Reading of Peircean Semiotic." Semiotiche, 2/04 [maggio 2004], pp. 49-68.

Colapietro V., (2006), "Engaged Pluralism: Between Alterity and

Sociality." The Pragmatic Century: Conversations with Richard J. Bernstein (Albany, NY: SUNY Press), pp. 39-68.

Colapietro V., (2009), "Habit, Competence, and Purpose." Forthcoming in The Transactions of the Charles S. Peirce Society. Calder AJ, Keane J, Manes F, Antoun N, Young AW (2000) Impaired recognition and experience of disgust following brain injury. Nature Neurosci 3: 1077–1078.

Carey DP, Perrett DI, Oram MW (1997) Recognizing, understanding and reproducing actions. In: Jeannerod M, Grafman J (eds) Handbook of neuropsychology. Vol. 11: Action and cognition. Elsevier, Amsterdam.

Carr L, Iacoboni M, Dubeau MC, Mazziotta JC, Lenzi GL (2003) Neural mechanisms of empathy in humans: a relay from neural systems for imitation to limbic areas. Proc Natl Acad Sci USA 100: 5497–5502.

Changeux JP, Ricoeur P (1998) La nature et la règle. Odile Jacob, Paris.

Cochin S, Barthelemy C, Roux S, Martineau J (1999) Observation and execution of movement: similarities demonstrated by quantified electroencephalograpy. Eur J Neurosci 11: 1839– 1842.

Chomsky Noam, (2017) Requiem for the American Dream

Chomsky Noam, (2016) Who Rules the World?

Chomsky Noam, (2010) How the World Works

Churchland, P.S. (1986), Neurophilosophy (Cambridge, MA: The MIT Press).

Churchland, P.S. & Ramachandran, V.S. (1993), 'Filling in: Why Dennett is wrong', in Dennett and His Critics:

Demystifying Mind, ed. B. Dahlbom (Oxford: Blackwell Scientific Press).

Churchland, P.S., Ramachandran, V.S. & Sejnowski, T.J. (1994), 'A critique of pure vision', in Large- scale Neuronal Theories of the Brain, ed. C. Koch & J.L. Davis (Cambridge, MA: The MIT Press).

Crick, F. (1994), The Astonishing Hypothesis: The Scientific Search for the Soul (New York: Simon and Schuster).

Crick, F. (1996), 'Visual perception: rivalry and consciousness', Nature, 379.

Crick, F. & Koch, C. (1992), 'The problem of consciousness', Scientific American, 267.

Craig AD (2002) How do you feel? Interoception: the sense of the physiological condition of the body. Nature Rev Neurosci 3: 655–666.

Damasio, A (2003a) Looking for Spinoza. Harcourt Inc. Damasio A (2003b) Feeling of emotion and the self. Ann NY Acad Sci 1001: 253–261.

d'Aquili, Eugene. "Senses of Reality in Science and Religion." Zygon 17, no 4 (1982)

d'Aquili, Eugene. "The Biopsychological Determinants of Religious Ritual Behavior." Zygon 10, no. 1 (1975)

d'Aquili, Eugene. "The Myth-Ritual Complex: A Biogenetic Structural Analysis." Zygon 18, no. 3 (1983)

d'Aquili, Eugene, and Andrew Newberg. The Mystical Mind: Probing the Biology of Religious Experience. Minneapolis: Fortress Press, 1999.

Daly DD. 1958. Ictal affect. Am J Psychiatry.

Damasio, A. (1994) Descartes' Error: Emotion, Reason and the Human Brain. New York, Putnams.

Damasio, A. (1999) The Feeling of What Happens: Body, Emotion and the Making of Consciousness. London, Heinemann.

Darwin, C. (1859) On the Origin of Species by Means of Natural Selection. London, Murray.

Darwin, C. (1871) The Descent of Man and Selection in Relation to Sex. London, John Murray.

Darwin, C. (1872) The Expression of the Emotions in Man and Animals. London, John Murray; also published 1965, Chicago, University of Chicago Press.

Dawkins, M.S. (1987) Minding and mattering. In C. Blakemore and S. Greenfield (eds) Mindwaves. Oxford, Blackwell, 151-60.

Dawkins, R. (1976) The Selfish Gene. Oxford, Oxford University Press; a new edition, with additional material, was published in 1989.

Dawkins, R. (1986) The Blind Watchmaker. London, Longman.

Di Pellegrino G, Fadiga L, Fogassi L, Gallese V, Rizzolatti G (1992) Understanding motor events: A neurophysiological study. Exp Brain Res 91: 176–80.

Deikman, A.J. (2000) A functional approach to mysticism. Journal of Consciousness Studies 7(11-12), 75-91.

Delmonte, M.M. (1987) Personality and meditation. In M. West (ed.) The Psychology of Meditation. Oxford, Clarendon Press, 118-32.

Dennett, D.C. (1987) The Intentional Stance. Cambridge, MA, MIT Press.

Dennett, D.C. (1988) Quining qualia. In A.J. Marcel and E. Bisiach (eds)

Consciousness in Contemporary Science. Oxford, Oxford University Press, 42-77.

Dennett, D.C. (1991) Consciousness Explained. Boston, MA, and London, Little, Brown and Co.

Dennett, D.C. (1995a) Darwin's Dangerous Idea. London, Penguin.

Dennett, D.C. (1995b) The unimagined preposterousness of zombies. Journal of Consciousness Studies 2(4), 322-6.

Dennett, D.C. (1995c) Cog: steps towards consciousness in robots. In T. Metzinger (ed.) Conscious Experience. Thorverton, Devon, Imprint Academic, 471-87.

Dennett, D.C. (1995d) The path not taken. Behavioral and Brain Sciences 18, 252-3; commentary on N. Block, On a confusion about a function of consciousness. Behavioral and Brain Sciences 18, 227.

Dennett, D.C. (1996a) Facing backwards on the problem of consciousness. Journal of Consciousness Studies 3(1), 4-6.

Dennett, D.C. (1996b) Kinds of Minds: Towards an Understanding of Consciousness. London, Weidenfeld & Nicolson.

Dennett, D.C. (1997) An exchange with Daniel Dennett. In J. Searle (ed.) The Mystery of Consciousness. New York, New York Review of Books, 115-19.

Dennett, D.C. (1998) The myth of double transduction. In S.R. Hameroff, A.W. Kaszniak and A. C. Scott (eds) Toward a Science of Consciousness: The Second Tucson Discussions and Debates. Cambridge, MA, MIT Press, 97-107.

Dennett, D.C. (1998b) Brainchildren: Essays on Designing Minds. Cambridge, MA, MIT Press.

Dennett, D.C. (2001) The fantasy of first person science. Debate with D. Chalmers, Northwestern University, Evanston, IL, February 2001.

Dennett, D.C. (2003) Freedom Evolves. New York, Penguin.

Dennett, D.C. and Kinsbourne, M. (1992) Time and the observer: the where and when of consciousness in the brain. Behavioral and Brain Sciences 15, 183-247, including commentaries and authors' responses.

Dewey J., (1911 [1977]), "Epistemological Realism: The Alleged Ubiquity of the Knowledge Relation." Journal of Philosophy, VIII, 20 (September 28, 1911).

Dewhurst, Kenneth, and A. W. Beard. "Sudden Religious Conversions in Temporal Lobe Epilepsy." British Journal of Psychiatry 117 (1970)

Dewhurst K, Beard AW. Sudden religious conversions in temporal lobe epilepsy. 1970 Epilepsy Behav 2003

Devinsky O, Lai G. Spirituality and religion in epilepsy. Epilepsy Behav 2008.

Devinsky, O., Morrell, MJ, Vogt, BA. (1995) 'Contribution of anterior cingulate cortex to behavior', Brain, 118.

Douglas Stone A., Chapter 24, The Indian Comet, in the book Einstein and the Quantum, Princeton University Press, Princeton, New Jersey, 2013.

E. Horvitz, "One Hundred Year Study on Artificial Intelligence: Reflections and Framing," ed: Stanford University, 2014.

Einstein A. (1925). "Quantentheorie des einatomigen idealen Gases". Sitzungsberichte der Preussischen Akademie der Wissenschaften.

Eckhart Meister, Selected Writings

Egidi R., ed. (1999), "Von Wright and 'Dante's Dream': Stages in a Philosophical Pilgrim's Progress", in In Search of a New Humanism: the Philosophy of G.H. von Wright, ed. by R. Egidi, Kluwer, Dordrecht.

Fadiga L, Fogassi L, Pavesi G, Rizzolatti G (1995) Motor facilitation during action observation: a magnetic stimulation study. J Neurophysiol 73: 2608–2611.

Fogassi L, Gallese V, Fadiga L, Rizzolatti G (1998) Neurons responding to the sight of goal directed hand/arm actions in the parietal area PF (7b) of the macaque monkey. Soc Neurosci Abs 24:257.5.

Frith U, Frith CD (2003) Development and neurophysiology of mentalizing. Philos Trans R Soc Lond B Biol Sci 358: 459.

Farah, M.J. (1989), 'The neural basis of mental imagery', Trends in Neurosciences, 10.

Finlay BL, Darlington RB (1995) Linked regularities in the development and evolution of mammalian brains. Science 268.

Freud, S. "The Interpretation of Dreams", 1900

Freud, S. "Selected papers on hysteria and other psychoneuroses" Journal of Nervous and Mental Disease 1909.

Freud, S. "The Origin and Development of Psychoanalysis", 1910

Freud, S. "Psychopathology of everyday life", 1914

Freud, S. "Beyond the Pleasure Principle", 1920

Frith, C.D. & Dolan, R.J. (1997), 'Abnormal beliefs: Delusions and memory', Paper presented at the May,

1997, Harvard Conference on Memory and Belief.

Gay, Volney, ed. Neuroscience and Religion. Plymouth, UK: Lexington Books, 2009.

Gazzaniga, M. S. (1985). The social brain. New York: Basic Books.

Gazzaniga, M.S. (1993), 'Brain mechanisms and conscious experience', Ciba Foundation Symposium, 174.

Geschwind N. "Behavioural changes in temporal lobe epilepsy". Psychol Med. 1979.

Gellhorn, E., Kiely, W.F. "Mystical states of consciousness: neurophysiological and clinical aspects." J Nerv Ment Dis. 1972;154:399-405.

Gilbert SL, Dobyns WB, Lahn BT (2005) Genetic links between brain development and brain evolution. Nat Rev Genet 6.

Gray JA. The Psychology of Fear and Stress. 2nd ed. New York, NY: Cambridge University Press; 1988.

Gloor, P. (1992), 'Amygdala and temporal lobe epilepsy', in The Amygdala: Neurobiological Aspects of Emotion, Memory and Mental Dysfunction, ed J.P. Aggleton (New York: Wiley-Liss).

Greenspan, S. I. and S. G. Shanker (2004). The first idea: How symbols, language, and intelligence evolved from our early primate ancestors to modern humans. Cambridge, MA: Da Capo Press.

Grady, D. (1993), 'The vision thing: Mainly in the brain', Discover, June.

Gallagher HL, Frith CD (2003) Functional imaging of 'theory of mind'. Trends Cogn Sci 7: 77.

Gallese V, Fogassi L, Fadiga L, Rizzolatti G (2002) Action representation and the inferior parietal lobule. In: Prinz W, Hommel B (eds) Attention & Performance XIX. Common mechanisms in perception and action. Oxford University Press, Oxford.

Gallese V, Keysers C, Rizzolatti G (2004) A unifying view of the basis of social cognition. Trends Cogn Sci 8: 396–403.

Gangitano M, Mottaghy FM, Pascual-Leone A (2001) Phase specific modulation of cortical motor output during movement observation. NeuroReport 12: 1489–1492.

Gangitano M, Mottaghy FM, Pascual-Leone A (2004) Modulation of premotor mirror neuron activity during observation of unpredictable grasping movements. Eur J Neurosci 20: 2193– 2202.

Goldman AI, Sripada CS (2004) Simulationist models of face-based emotion recognition. Cognition 94: 193–213.

Grèzes J, Costes N, Decety J (1998) Top-down effect of strategy on the perception of human biological motion: a PET investigation. Cogn Neuropsychol 15: 553–582.

Grèzes J, Armony JL, Rowe J, Passingham RE (2003) Activations related to "mirror" and "canonical" neurones in the human brain: an fMRI study. Neuroimage 18: 928–937.

Gross CG, Rocha-Miranda CE, Bender DB (1972) Visual properties of neurons in the inferotemporal cortex of the macaque. J Neurophysiol 35: 96–111.

Hari R, Forss N, Avikainen S, Kirveskari S, Salenius S, Rizzolatti G (1998) Activation of human primary motor cortex during action observation: a neuromagnetic study.

Proc. Natl Acad Sci USA 95: 15061–15065.

Hardy, G. H. (1940). Ramanujan. Cambridge: Cambridge University Press.

Hall, Daniel, Keith Meador, and Harold Koenig. "Measuring Religiousness in Health Research: Review and Critique." Journal of Religion and Health 47, no. 2 (2008)

Harris, Sam, Jonas Kaplan, Ashley Curiel, Susan Bookheimer, Marco Iacoboni, and Mark Cohen. "The Neural Correlates of Religious and Nonreligious Belief." PLoS One 4, no. 10 (October 1, 2009)

Halgren, E. (1992), 'Emotional neurophysiology of the amygdala within the context of human cognition', in The Amygdala: Neurobiological Aspects of Emotion, Memory and Mental Dysfunction, ed J.P. Aggleton (New York: Wiley-Liss).

Halligan PW, Fink GR, Marshal JC, Vallar G. 2003. Spatial cognition: evidence from visual neglect. Trends Cogn Sci.

Handbook of Emotions, Edited by Michael Lewis, Jeannette M. Haviland-Jones, and Lisa Feldman Barrett, The Guilford Press; 3rd edition (2010).

Haggard, P., Clark, S. and Kalogeras,]. (2002) Voluntary action and conscious awareness, Nature Neuroscience 5, 382-5. Haggard, P., Newman, C. and Magno, E. (1999) On the perceived time of voluntary actions. British Journal of Psychology 90, 291-303.

Hameroff, S.R. and Penrose, R. (1996) Conscious events as orchestrated space-time selections. Journal of Consciousness Studies 3(1), 36-53; also reprinted in J. Shear (ed.) (1997) Explaining Consciousness-The Hard Problem. Cambridge, MA, MIT Press, 177-95.

Hardcastle, V.G. (2000) How to understand theN in NCC. InT. Metzinger (ed.) Neural Correlates of Consciousness. Cambridge, MA, MIT Press, 259-64.

Harding, D.E. (1961) On Having no Head: Zen and the Re-Discovery of the Obvious. London, Buddhist Society.

Hardy, A. (1979) The Spiritual Nature of Man: A Study of Contemporary Religious Experience. Oxford, Clarendon Press.

Hamad, S. (1990) The symbol grounding problem. Physica D 42, 335-46.

Hamad, S. (2001) No easy way out. The Sciences 41(2), 36-42.

Harre, R. and Gillett, G. (1994) The Discursive Mind. Thousand Oaks, CA, Sage.

Haugeland, J. (ed.) (1997) Mind Design II: Philosophy, Psychology, Artificial

Intelligence. Cambridge, MA, MIT Press.

Hauser, M.D. (2000) Wild Minds: What Animals Really Think. New York, Henry Holt and Co.; London, Penguin.

Hearne, K. (1990) The Dream Machine. Northants, Aquarian.

Hebb, D.O. (1949) The Organization of Behavior. New York, Wiley.

Helmholtz, H.L.F. von (1856-67) Treatise on Physiological Optics.

Hess, EH (1975) "The role of pupil size in communication," Scientific American, 233(5), 110–12.

Heyes, C.M. (1998) Theory of mind in nonhuman primates. Behavioral and Brain Sciences 21, 101-48; with commentaries.

Heyes, C.M. and Galef, B.G. (eds) (1996) Social Learning in Animals: The Roots of Culture. San Diego, CA, Academic Press.

Hilgard, E.R. (1986) Divided Consciousness: Multiple Controls in Human Thought and Action. New York, Wiley.

Hocquette JF (2016) Is in vitro meat the solution for the future? Meat Science 120:

167–176

Hodgson, R. (1891) A case of double consciousness. Proceedings of the Society for Psychical Research 7, 221-58.

Hofstadter, D.R. (1979) Code!, Escher, Bach: An Eternal Golden Braid. London, Penguin.

Hofstadter, D.R. and Dennett, D.C. (eds) (1981) The Mind's I: Fantasies and Reflections on Self and Soul. London, Penguin.

Holland, J. (ed.) (2001) Ecstasy: The Complete Guide: A Comprehensive Look at the Risks and Benefits of

MDMA. Rochester, VT, Park Street Press.

Holmes, D.S. (1987) The influence of meditation versus rest on physiological arousal. In M. West (ed.) The Psychology of Meditation. Oxford, Clarendon Press, 81-103.

Holt, J. (1999) Blindsight in debates about qualia. Journal of Consciousness Studies 6(5), 54-71.

Horgan, J. (1994), 'Can science explain consciousness?', Scientific American, 271.

Holloway RL (1996) Evolution of the human brain. In: Lock A, Peters CR (eds) Handbook of human symbolic evolution. Oxford University Press, Oxford

Iacoboni M, Woods RP, Brass M, Bekkering H, Mazziotta JC, Rizzolatti G (1999) Cortical mechanisms of human imitation. Science 286: 2526–2528.

Iacoboni M, Koski LM, Brass M, Bekkering H, Woods RP, Dubeau MC, Mazziotta JC, Rizzolatti G (2001) Reafferent copies of imitated actions in the right superior temporal cortex. Proc Natl Acad Sci USA 98: 13995–13999.

Jeannerod M (1988) The neural and behavioural organization of goal-directed movements. Clarendon Press, Oxford.

Johnson-Frey SH, Maloof FR, Newman-Norlund R, Farrer C, Inati S, Grafton ST (2003) Actions or hand-objects interactions? Human inferior frontal cortex and action observation. Neuron 39: 1053–1058.

Jackson, F. (1982) Epiphenomenal qualia. Philosophical Quarterly 32, 127-36.

James, W. (1890) The Principles of Psychology (2 volumes). London, Macmillan.

James, W. (1902) The Varieties of Religious Experience: A Study in Human Nature. New York and London, Longmans, Green and Co.

Jansen, K. (2001) Ketamine: Dreams and Realities. Sarasota, FL, Multidisciplinary Association for Psychedelic Studies.

Jay, M. (ed.) (1999) Artificial Paradises: A Drugs Reader. London, Penguin.

Jaynes, J. (1976) The Origin of Consciousness in the Breakdown of the Bicameral Mind. New York, Houghton Mifflin.

Johnson, M.K. and Raye, C.L. (1981) Reality monitoring. Psychological Review 88, 67-85.

Kadim I, Mahgoub O, Baqir S et al. (2015) Cultured meat from muscle stem cells: a review of challenges and prospects. J Integr Agr 14: 222–233

Koski L, Iacoboni M, Dubeau MC, Woods RP, Mazziotta JC (2003) Modulation of cortical activity during different imitative behaviors. J Neurophysiol 89: 460–471.

Krolak-Salmon P, Henaff MA, Isnard J, Tallon-Baudry C, Guenot M, Vighetto A, Bertrand O, Mauguiere F (2003) An attention modulated response to disgust in human ventral anterior insula. Ann Neurol 53: 446–453.

Kandel, E. R. In Search of Memory: The Emergence of a New Science of Mind, W. W. Norton & Company (2007).

Kandel E. R. Schwartz JH, Jessel TM. Principles of neural sciences. New York; McGraw Hill, 2000.

Kanizsa, G. (1979), Organization In Vision (New York: Praeger).

Kaloupek DG, Scott JR, Khatami V. Assessment of coping strategies associated with syncope in blood donors. J Psychosom Res. 1985;29:207-214.

Kanwisher, N. (2001) Neural events and perceptual awareness. Cognition 79, 89-113; also reprinted inS. Dehaene (ed.) The Cognitive Neuroscience of Consciousness. Cambridge, MA, MIT Press, 89-113.

Kapleau, Roshi P. (1980) The Three Pillars of Zen: Teaching, Practice, and Enlightenment (revised edn). New York, Doubleday.

Karn, K. and Hayhoe, M. (2000) Memory representations guide targeting eye movements in a natural task. Visual Cognition 7, 673-703.

Kasamatsu, A. and Hirai, T. (1966) An electroencephalographic study on the Zen meditation (zazen). Folia Psychiatrica et Neurologica Japonica 20, 315-36.

Kaiserman-Abramof, I. R., Graybiel, A. M., & Nauta, W. J. (1980). The thalamic projection to cortical area 17 in a congenitally anophthalmic mouse strain. Neuroscience, 5, 41–52.

Kanold, P. O., Kara, P., Reid, R. C., & Shatz, C. J. (2003). Role of subplate neurons in functional maturation of visual cortical columns. Science, 301, 521–525.

Kennedy, H., & Dehay, C. (1988). Functional implications of the anatomical organization of the callosal projections of visual areas V1 and V2 in the macaque monkey. Behav. Brain Res., 29, 225–236.

Kentridge, R.W. and Heywood, C.A. (1999) The status of blindsight. Journal of Consciousness Studies 6(5), 3-11.

Kihlstrom, J.F. (1996) Perception without awareness of what is perceived, learning without awareness of what is learned. In M. Velmans (ed.) The Science of Consciousness. London, Routledge, 23-46.

Kollerstrom, N. (1999) The path of Halley's comet, and Newton's late apprehension of the law of gravity. Annals of Science 56, 331-56.

Kosslyn, S.M. (1980) Image and Mind. Cambridge, MA, Harvard University Press.

Kosslyn, S.M. (1988) Aspects of a cognitive neuroscience of mental imagery. Science 240, 1621-6.

Kinsbourne, M. (1995), 'The intralaminar thalamic nucleii', Consciousness and Cognition, 4.

Kjaer, Troels, Camilla Bertelsen, Paola Piccini, David Brooks, Jorgen Alving, and Hans Lou. "Increased Dopamine Tone during Meditation- Induced Change of Consciousness." Cognitive Brain Research 13, no. 2 (April 2002)

Kölmel HW. 1985. Complex visual hallucinations in the hemianopic field. J Neurol Neurosurg Psychiatry.

Koenig, Harold. "Research on Religion, Spirituality, and Mental Health: A Review." Canadian Journal of Psychiatry 54, no. 5 (May 2009)

Koenig, Harold, ed. Handbook of Religion and Mental Health. San Diego, CA: Academic Press, 1998

Kraepelin E. Psychiatry: A Textbook for Students and Physicians. New York, NY: Science History Publications; 1990.

Lauglin, Charles, John McManus, and Eugene d'Aquili. Brain, Symbol, and Experience. 2nd ed. New York: Columbia University Press, 1992

Lakoff, G. and M. Johnson (1999). Philosophy in the flesh. Basic Books: New York.

LeDoux, J. E. (1996). The emotional brain. New York: Simon & Schuster.

LeDoux, J.E. (1992), 'Emotion and the amygdala', in The Amygdala:

Neurobiological Aspects of Emo- tion, Memory and Mental Dysfunction, ed J.P. Aggleton (New York: Wiley-Liss).

Levin, D.T. and Simons, D.J. (1997) Failure to detect changes to attended objects in motion pictures. Psychonomic Bulletin and Review 4, 501-6.

Levine,J. (1983) Materialism and qualia: the explanatory gap. Pacific Philosophical Quarterly 64, 354-61.

Levine,J. (2001) Purple Haze: The Puzzle of Consciousness. New York, Oxford University Press. Levine, S. (1979) A Gradual Awakening. New York, Doubleday.

Levinson, B.W. (1965) States of awareness during general anaesthesia. British Journal of Anaesthesia 37, 544-6.

Lewicki, P., Czyzewska, M. and Hoffman, H. (1987) Unconscious acquisition of complex procedural knowledge. Journal of Experimental Psychology: Learning, Memory and Cognition 13, 523-30.

Lewicki, P., Hill, T. and Bizot, E. (1988) Acquisition of procedural knowledge about a pattern of stimuli that cannot be articulated. Cognitive Psychology 20, 24-37.

Lewicki, P., Hill, T. and Czyzewska, M. (1992) Nonconscious acquisition of information. American Psychologist 47, 796-801.

Manthey S, Schubotz RI, von Cramon DY (2003). Premotor cortex in observing erroneous action: an fMRI study. Brain Res Cogn Brain Res 15: 296–307.

Mesulam MM, Mufson EJ (1982) Insula of the old world monkey. III: Efferent cortical output and comments on function. J Comp Neurol 212: 38–52.

Naskar, Abhijit. "Homo: A Brief History of Consciousness", 2015

Naskar, Abhijit. "What is Mind?", 2016

Naskar, Abhijit. "Love, God & Neurons: Memoir of A Scientist who found himself by getting lost", 2016

Naskar, Abhijit. "Principia Humanitas", 2017

Naskar, Abhijit. "We Are All Black: A Treatise on Racism", 2017

Naskar, Abhijit. "Either Civilized or Phobic: A Treatise on Homosexuality", 2017

Naskar, Abhijit. "I Am The Thread: My Mission", 2017

Naskar, Abhijit. "The Bengal Tigress: A Treatise on Gender Equality", 2017

Naskar, Abhijit. "Morality Absolute", 2017

Naskar, Abhijit. "Build Bridges not Walls: In the name of Americana", 2018

Naskar, Abhijit. "Fabric of Humanity", 2018

Naskar, Abhijit. "Lives To Serve Before I Sleep", 2019

Naskar, Abhijit. "Citizens of Peace: Beyond the Savagery of Sovereignty", 2019

Naskar, Abhijit. "The Constitution of The United Peoples of Earth", 2019

Naskar, Abhijit. "Neurons Giveth, Neurons Taketh Away | Abhijit Naskar | TEDxIIMRanchi", 2019 https://www.youtube.com/watch?v=BNX-Q0ySm80

Naskar, Abhijit. "Mission Reality", 2019

Naskar, Abhijit. "Operation Justice: To Make A Society That Needs No Law", 2019

Naskar, Abhijit. "Every Generation Needs Caretakers: The Gospel of Patriotism", 2020

Naskar, Abhijit. "Revolution Indomable", 2020

Naskar, Abhijit. "Servitude is Sanctitude", 2020

Newberg, Andrew, and Jeremy Iversen. "The Neural Basis of the Complex Mental Task of Meditation: Neurotransmitter and Neurochemical Considerations." Medical Hypotheses 61, no. 2 (2003).

Newberg, Andrew. "How God Changes Your Brain: An Introduction to Jewish Neurotheology", CCAR Journal: The Reform Jewish Quarterly, Winter 2016.

Newberg, Andrew, and Stephanie Newberg. "A Neuropsychological Perspective on Spiritual Development." In Handbook of Spiritual Development in Childhood and Adolescence, edited by Eugene Roehlkepartain, Pamela King, Linda

Wagener, and Peter Benson. London: Sage Publications, Inc., 2005

Newberg, Andrew. "The Neurotheology Link An Intersection Between Spirituality and Health", Alternative and Complimentary Therapies, Vol 21 No 1, February 2015.

Newberg, Andrew, Nancy Wintering, Dharma Khalsa, Hannah Roggenkamp, and Mark Waldman. "Meditation Effects on Cognitive Function and Cerebral Blood Flow in Subjects with Memory Loss: A Preliminary Study." Journal of Alzheimer's Disease 20, no. 2 (2010)

Nash, M. (1995), 'Glimpses of the mind', Time.

Nesse RM. Proximate and evolutionary studies of anxiety, stress and depression: synergy at the interface. Neurosci Biobehav Rev. 1999;23:895-903.

Nicolelis, Miguel. (2011) "Beyond Boundaries: The New Neuroscience of Connecting Brains with Machines--- and How It Will Change Our Lives", Times Books

O'Hara, K. and Scutt, T. (1996) There is no hard problem of consciousness. Journal of Consciousness Studies 3(4), 290-302, reprinted in J. Shear (ed.) (1997) Explaining Consciousness. Cambridge, MA, MIT Press, 69-82.

O'Regan, J.K. (1992) Solving the "real" mysteries of visual perception: the world as an outside memory. Canadian Journal of Psychology 46, 461-88.

O'Regan, J.K. and Noe, A. (2001) A sensorimotor account of vision and visual consciousness. Behavioral and Brain Sciences 24(5), 883-917.

O'Regan, J.K., Rensink, R.A. and Clark,].]. (1999) Change-blindness as a result of "mudsplashes." Nature 398, 34.

Ornstein, R.E. (1977) The Psychology of Consciousness (2nd edn). New York, Harcourt.

Ornstein, R.E. (1986) The Psychology of Consciousness (3rd edn). New York, Pehguin.

Ornstein, R.E. (1992) The Evolution of Consciousness. New York, Touchstone.

Penfield W, Faulk ME (1955) The insula: further observations on its function. Brain 78: 445– 470.

Penrose, R. (1994), Shadows of the Mind (Oxford: Oxford University Press).

Penrose, R. (1989), The Emperor's New Mind: Concerning Computers, Minds and The Laws of Physics (Oxford: Oxford University Press).

Persinger, "'I would kill in God's name' role of sex, weekly church attendance, report of a religious experience and limbic lability" Perceptual and Motor Skills 1997.

Persinger "Experimental simulation of the God experience" Neurotheology 2003.

Persinger, M. A. (1993b). Personality changes following brain injury as a grief response to the loss of sense of self: Phenomenological themes as indices of local lability and neurocognitive restructuring as psycho- therapy. Psychological Reports, 72

Persinger, Corradini, Clement, Keaney, et al "Neurotheology and its convergence with neuroquantology" NeuroQuantology 2010.

Persinger, Koren and St-Pierre "The electromagnetic induction of mystical and altered states within the laboratory" Journal of Consciousness Exploration and Research 2010.

Persinger "Case report: A prototypical spontaneous 'sensed presence' of a sentient being and concomitant electroencephalographic activity in the clinical laboratory" Neurocase 2008.

Persinger and Saroka "Potential production of Hughlings Jackson's "parasitic consciousness" by physiologically-patterned weak transcerebral magnetic fields: QEEG and source localization" Epilepsy & Behavior 28 (2013).

Persinger. "The neuropsychiatry of paranormal experiences". J Neuropsychiatry Clin Neurosci 2001.

Persinger. "Neuropsychological bases of god beliefs", New York: Praeger, 1987

Persinger. "Temporal lobe epileptic signs and correlative behaviors displayed by normal populations", Journal of General Psychology, 1986

Perry BD, Pollard R. Homeostasis, stress, trauma, and adaptation. A neurodevelopmental view of childhood trauma. Child Adolesc Psychiatr Clin N Am. 1998;7:33.

Paré, D. & Llinás, R. (1995), 'Conscious and preconscious processes as seen from the standpoint of sleep-waking cycle neurophysiology', Neuropsychologia, 33.

P. S. de Laplace. Essai Philosophique sur les Probabilites [1814], in Academy des Sciences, Oeuvres Complotes de Laplace, Vol. 7, Gauthier-Villars, Paris (1886).

Perrett DI, Harries MH, Bevan R, Thomas S, Benson PJ, Mistlin AJ, Chitty AJ, Hietanen JK, Ortega JE (1989) Frameworks of analysis for the neural representation of animate objects and actions. J Exp Bio 146: 87–113.

Phillips ML, Young AW, Senior C, Brammer M, Andrew C, Calder AJ, Bullmore ET, Perrett DI, Rowland D, Williams SC, Gray JA, David AS (1997) A specific neural substrate for perceiving facial expressions of disgust. Nature 389: 495–498.

Phillips ML, Young AW, Scott SK, Calder AJ, Andrew C, Giampietro V, Williams SC, Bullmore ET, Brammer M, Gray JA (1998) Neural responses to facial and vocal expressions of fear and disgust. Proc R Soc Lond B Biol Sci 265: 1809–1817.

Puce A, Perrett D (2003) Electrophysiological and brain imaging of biological motion. Philosoph Trans Royal Soc Lond, Series B, 358: 435–445.

Ramachandran VS. Behavioral and magnetoencephalographic correlates of plasticity in the adult human brain. Proc Natl Acad Sci USA 1993; 90: 10413–20.

Ramachandran VS. Phantom limbs, neglect syndromes, repressed memories, and Freudian psychology. Int Rev Neurobiol 1994; 37: 291–333.

Ramachandran VS. Plasticity and functional recovery in neurology. Clin Med 2005; 5: 368–73.

Ramachandran VS, Hirstein W. The perception of phantom limbs. The D. O. Hebb lecture. Brain 1998; 121: 1603–30.

Ramachandran VS, Rogers-Ramachandran D, Cobb S. Touching the phantom limb. Nature 1995; 377: 489–90.

Ramachandran VS, Rogers-Ramachandran D. Phantom limbs and neural plasticity. Arch Neurol 2000; 57: 317–20.

Ramachandran VS, Rogers-Ramachandran D. It's all done with mirrors. Sci Am Mind 2007; 18: 16–9.

Ramachandran VS, Rogers-Ramachandran D. Sensations referred to a patient's phantom arm from another subjects intact arm: perceptual correlates of mirror neurons. Med Hypotheses 2008; 70: 1233–4.

Ramachandran VS, Rogers-Ramachandran D, Stewart M. Perceptual correlates of massive cortical reorganization. Science 1992; 258: 1159–60.

Rizzolatti G, Craighero L (2004) The mirror-neuron system. Annu Rev Neurosci 27: 169–192.

Rizzolatti G, Fogassi L, Gallese V (2001) Neurophysiological mechanisms underlying the understanding and imitation of action. Nature Rev Neurosci 2:661–670.

Rock I, Victor J. Vision and touch: an experimentally created conflict between the two senses. Science 1964; 143: 594–6.

Rose´n B, Lundborg G. Training with a mirror in rehabilitation of the hand. Scand J Plast Reconstr Surg Hand Surg 2005; 39: 104–8.

Royet JP, Plailly J, Delon-Martin C, Kareken DA, Segebarth C (2003) fMRI of emotional responses to odors: influence of hedonic valence and judgment, handedness, and gender. Neuroimage 20: 713–728.

Rozin R Haidt J and McCauley CR (2000) Disgust. In: Lewis M, Haviland-Jones JM (eds) Handbook of Emotion. 2nd Edition. Guilford Press, New York, pp 637–653.

Saxe R, Carey S, Kanwisher N (2004) Understanding other minds: linking developmental psychology and functional neuroimaging. Annu Rev Psychol 55: 87–124.

S. J. Russell and P. Norvig, Artificial intelligence: a modern approach (3rd edition): Prentice Hall, 2009.

Schienle A, Stark R, Walter B, Blecker C, Ott U, Kirsch P, Sammer G, Vaitl D (2002) The insula is not specifically involved in disgust processing: an fMRI study. Neuroreport 13: 2023–2026.

Showers MJC, Lauer EW (1961) Somatovisceral motor patterns in the insula. J Comp Neurol 117: 107–115.

Singer T, Seymour B, O'Doherty J, Kaube H, Dolan RJ, Frith CD (2004) Empathy for pain involves the affective but not the sensory components of pain. Science 303: 1157–1162.

Smith A (1759) The theory of moral sentiments (ed. 1976). Clarendon Press, Oxford.

S. N. Bose (1924). "Plancks Gesetz und Lichtquantenhypothese". Zeitschrift für Physik. 26 (1): 178–181.

Sprengelmeyer R, Rausch M, Eysel UT, Przuntek H (1998) Neural structures associated with recognition of facial expressions of basic emotions Proc R Soc Lond B Biol Sci 265: 1927–1931.

Strafella AP, Paus T (2000) Modulation of cortical excitability during action observation: a transcranial magnetic stimulation study. NeuroReport 11: 2289–2292.

Simonsen R (2015) Eating for the future: veganism and the challenge of in vitro meat. In: Stapleton P, Byers A (Hg). Biopolitics and utopia. Palgrave Macmillan, New York (2015), S 167–190

Tanaka K (1996) Inferotemporal cortex and object vision. Ann Rev Neurosci. 19: 109–140.

Tesla N. "My Inventions", 1919

T. R. Society, "Machine learning: the power and promise of computers that learn by example," ed. The Royal Society, 2017.

Tomasello M, Call J (1997) Primate cognition. Oxford University Press, Oxford.

Tremblay C, Robert M, Pascual-Leone A, Lepore F, Nguyen DK, Carmant L, Bouthillier A, Theoret H (2004) Action observation and execution: intracranial recordings in a human subject. Neurology. 63: 937–938.

Umilta MA, Kohler E, Gallese V, Fogassi L, Fadiga L, Keysers C, Rizzolatti G (2001) "I know what you are doing": a neurophysiological study. Neuron 32: 91–101.

Von Wright G.H., (1963), Norm and Action. A Logical Inquiry, Routledge & Kegan Paul, London.

Von Wright G.H., (1976), "Determinism and the Study of Man", in Essays on Explanation and Understanding, ed. by J. Manninen and R. Tuomela, Reidel, Dordrecht.

Von Wright G.H., (1977), "What is Humanism?", The Lindlay Lecture, University of Arkansas, Lawrence, Kansas.

Von Wright G.H., (1979), "Humanism and the Humanities", in Philosophy and Grammar, ed. by S. Kanger and S. Öhman, Reidel, Dordrecht, pp. 1-16. Reprinted in von Wright (1993).

Von Wright G.H., (1980), Freedom and Determination, North-Holland Publishing Co., Amsterdam.

Von Wright G.H., (1985), Of Human Freedom, The Tanner Lectures on Human Values,

Vol. VI, ed. by S. M. McMurrin, University of Utah Press, Salt Lake City, pp. 107-70. Reprinted in von Wright (1998).

Von Wright G.H., (1993), The Tree of Knowledge and Other Essays, Brill, Leiden.

Von Wright G.H., (1997), "Progress: Fact and Fiction", in The Idea of Progress, ed. by A. Burgen et al., W. de Gruyter, Berlin, pp. 1-18.

Von Wright G.H., (1998), In the Shadow of Descartes: Essays in the Philosophy of Mind, Kluwer, Dordrecht.